GOD WANTS YOU HEALED!

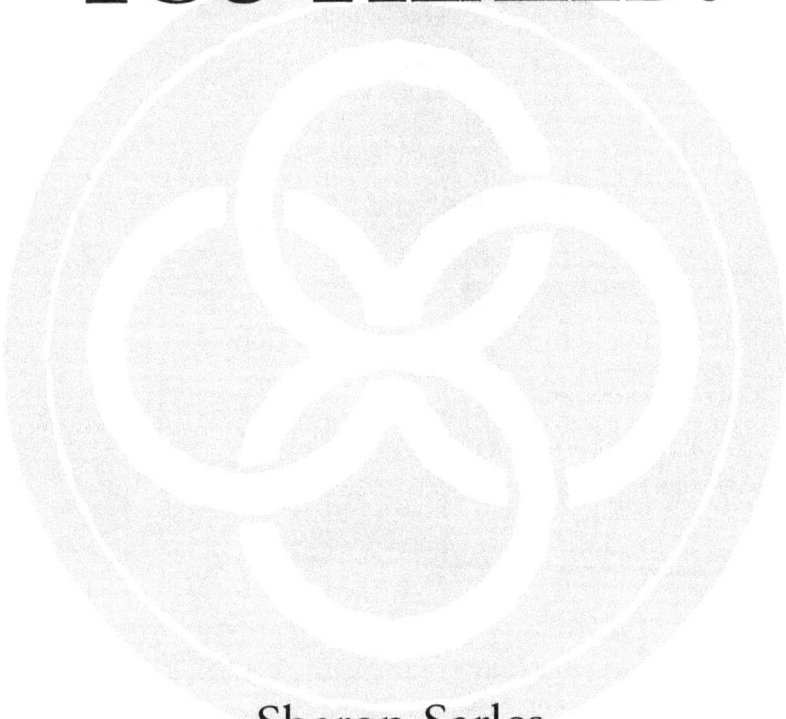

Sharon Sarles

Inquiries should be addressed to

ORGANIZATIONAL STRATEGIES
P.O. Box 971
Austin, Texas 78630
www.greatshalom.org

First Printing 2009

Quotations are from KJV, AV, unless otherwise noteed.

Sarles, Sharon
God Wants You Healed

     p.   cm.

1. Christian Life. 2. Healing —Faith.

Although information herein is based on the author's extensive
experience and knowledge, it is not intended to substitute for the
services of a qualified professional.

Printed in the United States of America
at Morgan Printing in Austin, Texas

TABLE OF CONTENTS

Introduction

Want you to receive God's healing. I want your children healed. I want healing to spread out; I want God's kingdom, God's way of doing things to spread out and deepen all around, all over earth, and become the settled way it is done here on earth.

I want people to embrace God's good gifts. I want people to see the gifts, wrapped up and topped with pretty bows; not missed, overlooked, and invisible.

I want children to skip free, to beam big smiles, to have their tongues loosed to praise, sing, and inquire. I want families to stop being bent low with grief, care, and pain. I want people to breathe free after the suffocation of resignation to sickness, brokenness, and creeping death.

More than this, God wants it.

Yes, God always wants everyone healed. I know this for sure. This is what I'm called to tell you. I suppose I could argue in the academic manner, but I don't think that would be effective. I know, I feel, I see in the Word of God, and I feel called to share: God wants to heal. But it is academic to explain about everyone. Let's get very real: God wants to heal you.

In the same way that God wants everyone saved He wants them healed.. We are used to thinking that God wants everyone saved, everyone to be forgiven of sins, brought close to God and given a fresh start and a new, good life. We know from 2 Peter 3:9 that God is not willing that any should perish, but that all come to repentance. Yet, we know that not everyone gets saved.

WE probably know some who do accept justification do not always enjoy all the benefits of salvation because they choose not to Some people do repent enough to ask God to forgive their sins, but stop there. they have become justified; it is just as if they never sins, but many do not go on to accept all that salvation has for them. They are justified, but don't go on to be sanctified, made holy. Their sins might be forgiven, but their mind is not transformed. If their mind is not transformed, you can bet their life is not completely transformed. But salvation is for the whole of life. If someone does not experience salvation in all of their life, it is not because that is God's will!

Jesse DuPlantis is now a well known preacher. He flies around to meetings in his own plane. He is on television and radio. He does a lot of good stuff. In his hometown he is particularly well known for his charity. Most of all he is known for his joyful message. He is so funny. You laugh when he preaches. Brother Jesse was saved while he was a rock and roll singer. What would have happened if he had accepted salvation just enough to be forgiven of his sins? What if he just continued to be a rock and roll singer? Of course it is possible for someone to be fully saved and a professional musician, but in this case, he was called to the ministry. Would he have had the wonderful lifestyle and the joy he has now if he just took salvation's first step? Somehow I doubt it. Forgive me Brother Jesse for using you as an example. It is just that people can see what life would be like as a saved person but living mostly in honky-tonks a honky-tonk life. Similarly, since he travels around the country and world, people know how blessed, how joyful, how fun he is.

Going all the way with God is SO much better than going just a little ways.. We see this in salvation. Why can't we see that salvation includes a great deal more than just justification? Healing is part of salvation.

Going all the way in faith on healing will be so much better than hemming and hawing at the beginning or some where in the middle. It works in salvation, in identifying yourself as a Christian. It works in all parts of the Christian life. It works in healing too.

Are you afraid? Fear not! Isn't this what God says to us? Why be afraid of our Father, our Redeemer, the one who is closer to us than a brother? Why hide from the Creator? Why shy away from the touch of love that will heal?

One of the greatest tricks of the enemy is to make us afraid to step out on God's word—"in case it doesn't work." Then our reputation will be ruined. Then our faith will be hurt. Then people won't believe God. Is that so? People *already* don't believe God. Our faith is *already* hurt when we believe less than the truth, or the lie that God doesn't want to heal you. . Our reputation is *already* lacking if we do not have demonstration. Better to trust in God. Better to step out learning how to walk than to be afraid and never try to walk. All I am saying is as a believer, as a child of God, and a disciple you are specifically told that God has healed you and that you are to pray for others and they will be healed. It is part of the Great Commission. It is part of our family culture. It is the kingdom, into which we have been transformed.

So accept it: God wants you healed!

CHAPTER ONE

God Always Wants To Heal You — And Your Children.
We Know This From Jesus' Life And Ministry

We all know that Jesus healed people. What keeps Him from healing now? Some people do teach that healing is not for today, but what I read is that Jesus is the same yesterday, today, and forever (Hebrews 13:8).

Someone came to Jesus and said, I know you can, but will you?" Jesus said, "I will." (Mark 1:40-41)

There is no reason to doubt that God wants you healed. One person did once before, and Jesus answered him:

Mark 1:39-41

40 And there came a leper to him [Jesus}, beseeching him, and kneeling down to him, and saying unto him, If thou wilt, thou canst make me clean.

41 And Jesus, moved with compassion, put forth his hand, and touched him, and saith unto him" I will; be thou clean ".

Leprosy was a dread disease, like AIDs is today. Jesus said, "Yes!", He does want to heal. We have shown many ways why we should trust that God wants us healed.
Let us go to God. Let us kneel down. Let us talk to him. Let us believe what God says to us. Let us thank him. Let us speak what God speaks, pray as Jesus and Paul prayed. Let us minister like Peter. God wants healing. Jesus said "Be clean." "Be whole" "Be whole." Let us receive, take hold of, (*lambanw* is the Greek word and it is an active taking hold of, not a passive

reception) let us firmly grasp of this Word. Let us believe and speak this word. Let this word live in us.

Jesus went about doing good, healing people. In several places it says that "he healed them all." Jesus is still the same.

Some people say, "Well, only one guy at the pool of Siloam got healed." Fine, maybe so, but nowhere does it say that Jesus didn't WANT to heal everyone else. Some people looked to the pool, the angel, the tradition, the temple. One person accepted healing from Jesus.

Even he had to be coaxed. "Do you want to be healed?" Jesus asked. Out from his mouth came a distraction: "I have no man to let me down into the water." Jesus said, "Rise, take up thy bed and walk." John 5:7&8

Perhaps no one else looked at Jesus. Perhaps no one else listened to Jesus. Perhaps others turned away when he approached them. We do know that this fellow heard, responded to, and obeyed Jesus. "And immediately the man was made whole, and took up his bed, and walked" v.9a

We do not, absolutely do not, have any stories of people coming to Jesus, looking to him for healing, asking for help and Him turning them away.

Jesus says to you today: "Do you want to be healed?" He has made provision. He is present. He is powerful. He is willing. Look to him. Call to him. Are you by the pool at the temple? If he spoke to you, would you obey? Look to Jesus! Thank Him for his great work for you.

Healing Stories

*I*t was suggested to me that if would help the reader if they knew some of my story; that some of the comments I make about healing would be clearer if they know the story of healings that my family has been through. Therefore, I am going to intersperse healing stories between the chapters, not because I am some sort of model, or because my experiences prove how great I am—far from it—but in order to give you an idea that what I say is true. Of course, in reality, the Word of God is far truer than the accounts of my history. However, telling you about my experience may encourage you to more deeply consider the Word.

I am only just learning, but I will relate what has happened to me.

Healing of an Allergic Reaction

When I was fifteen and a Sophomore in High School I experienced a dramatic healing. I was practicing my bugle, for the Belles' Drum and Bugle Corps, facing into the full clothes closet, so as not to torture the whole neighborhood. An allergic reaction arose so that my lip swelled up very badly. I looked in the mirror. My face was red, my lip was swollen. My legs were starting to itch. Red welts came up. Normally the reaction took at least overnight to subside. It was clear that in a few minutes I would not be able to play the bugle. I commanded the reaction to stop in the name of Jesus and my lip to go down. I returned to my playing. Within one song, my lip was back to normal and my legs, fine.

I had a lot of allergy problems when I was in high school in Houston. Much later, I conquered most of them through better health, but this was one of several instances of instantaneous healing that I had when I was a teenager that confirmed my perhaps early belief in healing. By the time this incident occurred I must have read Kenneth Hagin's booklet "The Authority of the Believer." It had to have been with that understanding that I would have commanded the allergic reaction to go away.

CHAPTER TWO

God Always Wants to Heal You. We Know This From Jesus' Work on the Cross, His Death and Resurrection.

"Surely/ firmly/truly, we know that He bore our sickness and carried away our pain." Isaiah 53: 4

(translated literally from Hebrew)

Not only is this plain Hebrew, but also we know this is the correct interpretation of the Isaiah scripture, for it is quoted in Matthew, clearly in the context of healing:

Matthew 8:16&17
And when evening had come, they brought to Him any who were demon-possessed; and He cast out the spirits with a word, and healed all who were ill
17 in order that what was spoken through Isaiah the prophet might be fulfilled, saying, "He himself took our infirmities, and carried away our disease."

We know also from I Peter 2:24: "By His wounds you were healed." The context is indeed, total healing, not just bodily, but the wider of the chapters is one of complete practicality. Peter is dealing with common, everyday matters, not things that could be figurative or vague. It is evident that Peter is alluding to Isaiah 53 : "no guile, relived not again" and then in v 24 " who his own self bare our sins in his own body on the tree, that we, being dead to sins, should live unto righteousness: by whose stripes ye were healed, v 25 For ye were as sheep going astray, but are now returned unto the Shepherd and the Bishop of your souls.

I Peter 2:24 & 25
Who his own self bare our sins in his own body on the tree, that
we, being dead to sins, should live unto righteousness: by whose
stripes ye were healed
For ye were as sheep going astray; but are now returned unto the
Shepherd and Bishop of your souls.

We are completely made whole. Bodily healing is included in our overall
healing. For those who may argue that we are called to suffer, please look
this scripture up and read it in context. We are called to suffer *persecution*
following Jesus, but Jesus took our sin and gave us shalom/well-being.
We are so healed that we can do as he did, and be patient when we are
buffeted for doing well. Jesus bore our grief, took away our sin. And the
same scripture goes on to say that that by his stripes, that is the flogging
he took at the hands of the Roman soldiers, we are healed. Further it says,
the chastisement necessary for our full shalom was upon him. Isaiah 53
says we are saved and healed by Jesus' suffering.

It is a sure and firm word, affirmed by three scriptures.

And by many many who have believed and received.

Take your stand on the sure word of God. Every word is sure. Your salvation is sure, if you have received and believed. Now receive the rest of your
salvation, the rest of your healing, the salvation of your body.

It is the plain word of God, witnessed to and explained—clearly and suc-
cinctly. Therefore I recommend simply sitting and soaking in these verses.
Why keep arguing when God has spoken? The thing to do is to bring your
mind into alignment with what you should now know. Reread, meditate,
study out these scriptures. Satisfy yourself. I think you will find it clear.

God wants you healed. We know this from the cross, death, and resurrection of Jesus.

At the last supper with His disciples, Jesus talks about what his death will
mean. In so doing, he instituted a memorial that would always be passed

down, always remembered, always teach about that meaning. He said:

> Mt 26:28 For this is my blood of the new covenant which is shed
> for many for the remission of sins,

The King James says "remission of sins" and today that makes it sound like this is a some particularly churchy (and therefore insignificant, stuff(do you mean insignificant stuff? Or insignificant and stuffy?) or hard to understand) version of forgiveness of sin. Actually the word is a*phesis,* meaning *freedom* or *pardon.* We know that we have been pardoned for our sins. Do we know that we are also free from our sins? Look, some people take communion, but fail to lay hold of the forgiveness signified by it. They accept churchiness but still worry about whether God forgives them. Yes, you know people like this. But what about *us* forgetting to lay hold of the freedom from sin? Yes, we know that "God is faithful and just to forgive our sin and cleanse us." I John 1:7 What about this: sickness is a result of sin. Yet, if we are free from sin, *aphesis,* then isn't healing contained in the New Covenant? Sure it is.

The communion service is a memorial of Jesus' work on the cross, exactly what Isaiah 53 is talking about. 4 "Surely he bore our sickness and carried our pain..... 5 By his stripes we are healed."

Of course, Jesus took not just our sickness, but all our sins.

> 5 He was wounded for our transgression, he was bruised for our
> iniquities: the chastisement for our *shalom*/wellbeing was upon
> him.... 6 and the LORD hath laid on him the iniquity of us all"

The work of the Messiah on the cross was more than taking away our sickness. Indeed, he took away our sin. The blood of bulls and goats could cover sin for a time, but only the blood of a Perfect Sacrifice can take away sin.

For some of us this is so repeatedly in our ears, that we forget what an astonishment it is. This is an astonishment for Jews. This is perhaps even a greater astonishment for Muslims. God knew this and says so right in this passage. Isaiah 52:14 indicates that the many are astonished. They expected a Messiah—but not like this. This didn't fit their pattern, like heaven is above the earth. The point here is not that the Messiah is not good looking, but instead that He is not what people were looking for. "He will be despised" (verse 3), means more like "He will be a rejection of the people"—something considered worthy of hasty dismissal. Others reject the idea of a suffering Messiah. We reject only His efficacy! This is what people have done with deliverance from sin and even more with healing: dismissed it, since it is an astonishment. Suggestion for last sentence: Because it is an astonishment people have dismissed deliverance from sin; and dismissed to an even greater degree healing.

But for those of us who see and understand, it is wonderfully astonishing, a marvel, and amazement even greater still. No wonder the prophet says next: "Sing!" (51:1) and "Ho! Everyone one that thirsteth!" (52:1). The Rock of Calvary flows out life for all who would receive it. I think the picture in Revelation 22:1 of the river of life flowing from the Throne and Lamb, with a tree with healing for nations is another picture of the same thing. Amazingly, God has purposed to give us so great a rescue!

And of course, unlike a sheep or goat that stays dead after being sacrificed, Jesus was raised from the dead, thereby purchasing a much greater salvation. It wasn't possible, of course, that Christ, the Son of God, the Prince of Life could be held by death Acts 2:24, Acts 3:15. Subsequently, those who testified of this resurrection themselves moved in power, prosperity, and healings (Act 4:23, 4.34, and Acts 5:15).

Today, one of the most quoted verses of Scripture, used in explaining salvation to people is Romans 10:9 "that if thou shalt confess with they mouth the Lord Jesus and shalt believe in thine heart that God hat raised him from the death, thou shalt be saved."
The fact that God raised Jesus from the dead was central to the Apostle Paul because this shows God's power to save from everything. Naturally, you can't be in worse trouble than dead. Yet death couldn't hold Jesus. And all your troubles went with him.

So your healing is taken care of.

Can it be that you can be saved, by God's grace and power, demonstrated through Jesus, but that somehow this grace and power doesn't extend to healing? Of course not. Could it be that Jesus' death on Calvary could be sufficient for pardon for sin, but not for sickness? Is it possible that Jesus' stripes were sufficient only for mental or spiritual healing? Satan, get away! The enemy who comes immediately to steal the Word will try, but we are not ignorant of his methods. NO! in all that we have said the clear meaning of the Hebrew (no matter the astonishment of academics for centuries), the clear meaning of the very world *salvation*, a translation of the word *shalom* meaning *total well being*, the very fact of Jesus literal death and literal resurrection, and the experience of the early church in proclaiming it all indicate clearly that your healing is bought, purchased, eternally secure, and provided for you. AMEN.

Healing of Blepharitis

Also when I was in high school I had blepharitis once too. It is just an inflammation of the edge of the eyelid. I prayed for healing for it, I think. But I still had it, and Mother took me to the eye doctor. He prescribed some medicine. When I returned home, I went into the bathroom, and got on my knees and seriously sought the Lord for healing, because for some reason I knew I couldn't take the medicine and felt I had a very short timeline to get well. When I came out of the bathroom, and went to my parents, they had to agree that my eye looked well and there was no reason to do anything further.

CHAPTER THREE

God Always Wants You Healed. We Know This From Jesus' and the Holy Spirit's Current Work.

Okay, so we have established that Jesus went about healing. He established that He is the same today, as he was yesterday, and will always be (Hebrews 13:8).

Yes, but He is not here today, you may say.

Is He not? Okay, so you don't see him. Where is Jesus today?

- In heaven making intercessions
- At the right hand of God
- Here by the Holy Spirit he sent
- In His Body.

  "Wherefore he is able also to save them to the uttermost that come unto God by him, seeing he ever liveth to make intercession for them." Hebrews 7:25

Where is Jesus? Jesus is in heaven praying. Intercession is praying for others. Jesus is praying for us. It is rather mind blowing, isn't it? What do you think He is praying? In I john 2:1 it says that Jesus advocates for us. It is true that everything Jesus did is a mediation between us and God, but this verse indicates to me that still, right now, in heaven, Jesus is still interceding for us. When we intercede for each other, we call it intercessory prayer.

If that is what Jesus is doing, what is he asking for on our behalf? My guess is that he would ask that we know, believe, and lay hold of his promises.

He is rooting for the children of God to be able to live out his commands, just as any father roots for, pulls for, watches with interest the efforts of his children. Yes, my guess is also that Jesus is asking for those who don't know him, who have not yet received his great gift, that they would be moved to do so. How much more, for us who do know him, would he be hoping we fully receive the gift? He is working to save us completely, wholly, to the outermost.

What good would it be if we took a wrapped Christmas gift from a rich man, but just looked at the pretty paper, and never opened it? What good would it be, if we left the present in the hand of the giver? It would be bad when someone slaps the gift out of the hand that is reaching out, trying to give the gift. It would also be bad when the gift is not opened. Or opened and not used. How sad for the giver!

Whatever Jesus is praying, the result is that we are saved to the uttermost. Not just barely saved. Not just pardoned to be pardoned again, but forgiven and cleanses. Set free and transformed to stay free. Not just rescued, but rooted and fruited, surrounded in *shalom*: total well-being, peace, health, prosperity, nothing missing nothing broken.

Saved to the uttermost must included healing.

> Ephesians 1: 19-23
> 19 And his incomparably great power for us who believe. That power is like the working of his mighty strength, 20 which he exerted in Christ when he raised him from the dead and seated him at his right hand in the heavenly realms, 21 far above all rule and authority, power and dominion, and every title that can be given, not only in the present age but also in the one to come. 22 And God placed all things under his feet and appointed him to be head over everything for the church, 23 which is his body, the fullness of him who fills everything in every way.

Right now Jesus is at the right hand of God. This means that he is seated as first officer of the king, like first mate to the captain. Kings are seated on their throne. God is on the highest throne in the universe. Jesus is his "right hand man." This means that Jesus is higher than any other authority, legitimate or not. He is above every name that can be named. Paul stretches his Greek and loads it down as much as can be to describe the high glory and deep significance of the power of redemption.

Jesus is at the right hand of the throne of God. This means that he is over everything—every, every, every thing. All things, without exception, are under his feet.

And we are seated with him. Ep 2: 6 And hath raised us up together, and made us sit together in heavenly places in Christ Jesus. After all we are his body, so (as Pastor Don Olson often says), even if we are callous on the little toe, we are still above the everything, the all things, the all that is under His feet. His Name is above every name. "Every name" includes the name of any disease, any foul spirit that causes un-ease, and any situation that stresses and vexes. The Name of Jesus, the name we call upon, alls upon and causes every other name to bow.

No wonder Paul says that we have been given the gift of knowing the mystery of His will (Ephesians 1:9) for it is astonishing. It is mind blowing. But why accept only gifts that are small enough to fit in with our expectations? So you expected a tie and God gives you a Ferrari. Is that reason to deny the car? Or park it? Receive it! (It is a Ferrari life!)

Where is Jesus? He is in the Spirit who is here on earth in his stead. For the Holy Spirit is the Spirit of Christ (R 8:9). And what is the Spirit doing?

John 16: 7- 15
7 Nevertheless I tell you the truth; It is expedient for you that I go away: for if I go not away, the Comforter will not come unto you; but if I depart, I will send him unto you.
8 And when he is come, he will reprove the world of sin, and of righteousness, and of judgment:
9 Of sin, because they believe not on me;
10 Of righteousness, because I go to my Father, and ye see me no more;

11 Of judgment, because the prince of this world is judged.

12 I have yet many things to say unto you, but ye cannot bear them now.

13 Howbeit when he, the Spirit of truth, is come, he will guide you into all truth: for he shall not speak of himself; but whatsoever he shall hear, that shall he speak: and he will shew you things to come.

14 He shall glorify me: for he shall receive of mine, and shall shew it unto you.

The Spirit came to show us Christ's intention, work, and ways, because we were so unlikely to understand without the Spirit's help. So, please allow me to point out, that one of the things that we are so unlikely to believe is God's provision for our healing. The Spirit is here to get our attention, draw us, convince us, help us. We need all this because, compared to God, we are not so bright. For instance, we think we understand about salvation, say it is for our whole life, but then don't realize we could be saved from sickness too. The Holy Spirit just has to teach us.

The King has been at rest in his throne, knowing his edict, his announced plan, will be accomplished. The Prince has returned from the battlefield and is given a throne next to his father. The work is finished. New subjects have been transferred from the kingdom of darkness into the kingdom of light. So now the Holy Spirit, like a self-effacing Queen, has been sent out to the nursery to be sure the new children in the family begin to understand what a great heritage they have.

If our new life is accomplished, if the work is finished, then all of it is. Healing is part of salvation. So it is that our healing is now spoken of in past tense. Now the Kings' heralds declares it. Now the Spirit leads us into walking in it. The Spirit, like a good mother in the nursery, coaxes us along, convinces us to try, pick us up when we fall, and points out the way.

Also, like a governor, the Spirit lives in us, as the royal family's representative in a colony. The Holy Spirit governs. If we submit ourselves to that government, enculture our lives in the Royal culture, we transform our minds and our bodies. Just are we are changed socially when we "hang out" with a "certain crowd" so we are changed as we live in union with the Holy Spirit. Similarly, milk is changed to yogurt through the colonization of a culture. We are changed like that, from one kind of person to another. I have seen people come in from the world, a mess in every way, who as they get the rest of their lives in order, find their health improves dramatically. So in this way all of us should be growing more like our eternal Father. It will be the Spirit also, who helps over the last step, into incorruptibility. It is the Spirit indeed who quickens, enlivens our bodies (Romans 8:9-11).

So where is the Spirit of Christ? Right in your heart, speaking to you about healing!

> John 14: 26 But the Comforter, which is the Holy spirit, whom the Father wills end in my name, he shall teach you all things, and bring all things to your remembrance, whatsoever I have said unto you.
> John 16:7 Nevertheless I tell you the truth; It is expedient for you that I go away: for if I go not away, the Comforter will not come unto you; but if I depart, I will send him unto you
> 13 Howbeit when he, the Spirit of truth is come, he will guide you into all truth: for he shall unto speak of himself; but whatsoever he shall hear, that shall he speak: and he will shew you things to come
> Romans 8:14 For as many as are led by the Spirit of God, they are the sons of God...
> 16 The Spirit itself beareth witness with our spirit, that we are the children of God:

No wonder the Spirit is the earnest, the down payment of our inheritance (Ephesians 1:14). The enlivening and the mind opening power is the first of the power that will raise us up to eternal, everlasting, incorruptible life also.

Where is Jesus? Jesus is also in His Body, the church (I Corinthians 12:13) and that body is supposed to be growing up just like Christ (Ephesians 4: 14 & 15). It is very clear what we are supposed to be doing. It is recorded in Mark 16: 14 that Jesus told the eleven, after correcting them for their unbelief and hardness of heart ,15 "that we should go into all the world, preaching the gospel… 18 and laying hands on the sick." Fortunately the words of promise follow directly: "and they shall recover."

Of course, we do know a number of instances of people in the past century who had healing ministries and in whose meetings many people were healed. Today there are thousands upon thousands of people who have been healed in such meetings, and often healed of serious conditions.

If you consult you own life and that of your believing friends, I am confident that you will discover numerous instances of answered prayers and some healings. It might be helpful to write these instances down, so that the next time you feel "really crummy" you can remember that you have experienced God's healing in the past.

My guess is that when you are faced with this scripture, you like me, first feels the hope and draw and aspiration to going around and praying for people and their being healed, but then when you put yourself in that picture, you recoil and say, "Oh no! How can that be! What if?!?" My experience tells me it is best not to think in that direction. In such cases it is better just to keep your eye on the word, cut off any other thoughts, and just be obedient. I remember one evening when I was finally back in a praise service after a long time and I was faced with a song that spoke to God as Lord. I had a lot of problems with the word Lord. I could have sat down and had a very long rant about the word Lord, but I chose to tell myself "shut up and sing." I am glad I did. The intervening years have been much happier because I made that choice. I have had a lot of experience being reasonable and searching out truth with reason. I have found that when you have a direct communiqué from the Truth, the most effective and efficient thing to do is to get on board and not dither at the gate.

So Jesus is triumphantly seated at the right hand of God the King of the Universe, interceding for us, represented by the Spirit in our hearts, and in us, the Body of Christ to whom he gives all the authority. When he was here, Jesus went about doing good and healing those who came to him. We say we are growing up to be like him. We might as well start toddling in this direction.

I Was Asked to Pray

In 1981. I was in Spokane taking a class on the Montessori Method of education. I was a young mother in my very early 20s. One of my classmates, a little older than I was, was a beautiful woman, very sophisticated and cool—and a Rajneesh devote. (For those of you not as old as I am, Rajneesh was a syncretistic teacher from India whose cult got into several kinds of serious and widely publicized trouble shortly after this incident. For a time, however, he had quite a few highly educated American followers.) This gal asked me to pray for her leg that was hurting her. I agreed, and prayed earnestly for her later in my room.

In a couple of days, she came back, quite glad, and related that indeed, she no longer hurt. Now, would I pray for the peace of Northern Ireland? Okay, I agreed. Back home in a small town in Alberta, I brought this concern to the altar at the church where I attended. That was not what we normally prayed for there in those days, but my friends there did pray with me. And I prayed when I could remember. It was only weeks before I heard on the news that some progress had been made.

CHAPTER FOUR

God Wants You Healed.
We Know This From The Grand Plan
of Replacing Curse with Blessing.

Freedom from sickness was obtained in the stripes, the cross, the death, and the resurrection of Jesus, *Yeshua* the Messiah. We also know that God wants us healed because God's plan of salvation is a blessing to overturn the curse of the fall.

God is a reverse the curse God.

You know, it is just not so great on earth right now. We have a story in the beginning of the book that explains why. If we have a garden, we have to weed it. Nobody thinks it is fine if we have only weeds and no vegetables. Nobody thinks it is fine that we have pain. When we hurt, we take medicine. On the other hand, we are not surprised. Everyone on earth knows that things don't always go as we would wish. Gardens get weeds. Bodies hurt. Bodies die. Sometimes we don't feel very close to God. We worry; we are bewildered; we know torment.

So we make garden hoes; we take aspirin; we try all manner of things.

The best fix would be something that addressed the root cause of the mess up. Fortunately, we have one. We accept that God has created a plan, a path back. We accept the reversal of the curse of sinfulness and separation from God. Why not then seek the same remedy for sickness and torment? It is available.

Why then do we not lay hold of the reverse of the curse of sickness as strongly as the reverse for the curse of sin? Is it that we think our sin is insignificant? Is it that sin is invisible? Or is it just that it is *our* sin we think is easily dealt with, but that other stuff....

Maybe we think sickness is real, but sin is not? Or maybe sin is just a bit weaker, so it is easier to lay hold of the reverse of sin? Look, sin is the cause of sickness, at the root. If we can believe for it to be taken away, why not believe for healing also?

Healing we know is significant, because we actually hurt. We feel terrible. I think maybe sin is perhaps worse, partly because we don't perceive it so much. However, it cripples us just as much. But sickness and disease really annoy us very much. It is hard to ignore. Why then do we not focus on claiming healing? Understand God's promises on healing? Preach and pray for healing?

Do we lose faith because people shame us, say bad things to us about seeking healing or might say bad things to us if they know we believed for healing but still seemed sick? Does our faith falter because we can see or feel sickness but not God?

Hmm, actually I don't see sickness. I feel and occasionally see the results of sickness. I do often feel God. I have sometimes seen *** What is it that I see? I see the results of God action in all of creation. I have had God answer my prayers. I have experienced getting healed miraculuously, instantaneously, as well as gradually. I have also often epxerinced not getting sick when others did. I have experiences others saying they feel better after we prayed. Numerous times I have known of healings that included both prudent health measures and prayer—results that far exceeded medicine's prognosis. I have been told of many case sof miraculous healings. Therefore I am not embarrassed to believe for healing.

There are, however, some arguments that have shamed me out of belief in the past. "Be reasonable!" I've been told. Reason would not have brought my grandson back to life. It wasn't my family's idea of reasonableness that kept me more healthy than they are. It was not reason that made me joyful after years of unhappiness. It was not reasonableness that kept me through dark hours or gave me unexpectedable blessings. It is not reason

27

that sustains me in years of more happiness than my friends can believe. It is faith in God.

BTW, not just faith. I have tried faith in the mind/ body connections. That works to some extent. I have tried faith in the Universal Mind. That works too. But faith in YHWH is unbeatable. That is my experience. God's echo is everywhere, but God himself is findable, interactive, and more real than reality.

Faith is not just determination. Faith is not just some mystic link to the divine principle. Faith is trust in, reliance in the sure promises and power of a Particular Person.

It is my intention to proclaim the word of faith, speaking the Word of God as well as I am able, and not to spend time on arguing. Nevertheless, please let me make some distinctions, so we can fully embrace the Word and will of God, and see some arguments as merely a "hath God said?"

One argument that allows people to turn aside from seeking healing is a platitude that sounds very pious. Indeed, it is true in one sense, but it becomes untrue depending on how it is used. I have heard : "God is on his throne" meaning : "Oh well, let's just resign ourselves." NO! God has given the earth to the sons of men (Ps 115:16). Jesus told us to cast out demons and lay hands on the sick and they will recover Mark 16: 17b & 18d&e). Why is it that my friends who were once so ready to do great things, cast out demons, and bring in the millennium, will now just lay back when healing is not manifest? If a demon laughed at you the first time you spoke to it, would you just lay back and say, "Well God is on his Throne"? No, you would redouble your effort. You would tell it to shut up and get out now. Let's not get so tired in praying for healing. I imagine God is on the Throne of Heaven. But where are you? Are you in the will of God? Are you going into all the world and proclaiming the gospel? What gospel? The gospel of full salvation? As you go, are you braving scary things manfully? This is what I take Mark 16:18a to mean ("they shall take up serpents; and if they drink any deadly thing, it shall not hurt them) that we should go bravely, in full confidence of God's help, for it seems silly to me to go get snakes; there are plenty of real poisons and figurative snakes in the way as it is. Are we laying hands on the sick? Are we casting out demons? Are we subduing/conquering what is wrong in this earth? Are we taking dominion/ruling? This is our task, not weakly laying back saying, "God is on His throne."

I want words and actions of faith, laying hold of The Blessing of Christ, not reasonable sounding stories about why we have the reverse.

There is a curse in the world. People are cursed. The world order is cursed. Genesis 3:17 says the very ground is cursed for Adam's sake. There is a blessing for those who listen and obey, outlined in Deuteronomy 28:1-14, but for those who will not listen and will not observe the commandments, there are curses. It is not as if God is some petulant alien child who curses people who do not agree with him, but rather a good parent who lays out the best way to live, knowing full well that opposite choices hold bad results. The law, then became a curse on top of the fall. (And even if you don't take the story of the fall literally it just doesn't matter as far as this argument is concerned : we find that we do wrong things and we find that when we are taught the right things it only makes matters worse, because, try as we might, we do wrong. Any one who has actually tried to live to a high moral standard, instead of just spouting spin to avoid such, knows this.)

However, clearly the curse was reversed. Paul's letter in Galatians talks about it directly. Galatians 3:18. Paul argues that the Galatians, Gentiles, are saved not through keeping the law, but through faith, just as Abraham was referring to : It was reckoned to him as righteousness Genesis 15:6. So we received the blessing of Abraham (Galatians 3:14) and the promises were made to Abraham and his seed, singular, thus meaning Christ (v16). So in Christ we have justification and all the great promises made before.

Now, the blessings on Abraham were great. Primarily Paul means, " It was accounted to him for righteousness" (Genesis 15:6) because that is what Paul is talking about, being righteous without keeping the law. But Abraham is also blessed with God backing him up (bless those who bless you , I will bless Genesis 12:2) and with being blessing to the whole world Gen 12: 2 & 3. Also in Gen 13, Abraham was given the whole land. I take this figuratively as well as literally. Abraham was given the land we now call the Middle East. I personally am more interested in taking control of my life. I'll let Abraham's literal seed literally live in the literal land. I am interested in seeing the promises of God fulfilled in my metaphorical land, my life. Abraham was blessed also with physical riches and finally with a child well into old age. The point is that Abraham was blessed exceedingly, not just in relationship to God but in all ways in life. So we are blessed with Abraham's blessing, not only in relationship to God but in all ways in life—by faith. This is the gospel.

But we still see the effects of the curse. We still see sickness. We still see a broken world order. We still see the planet having great difficulty. What is up? My understanding is that while we have the curse reversed to blessing positionally, we must take it, like you take a present, open it up, and use it, so we have it possessionally.

Christ has redeemed us from the curse that the blessing of Abraham, that is, being justified by faith, may come on us (Gal 3: 13 & 14). The Curse is off; blessing is on. This is the center of the gospel. Let us not frustrate the grace of God.

The end of the gospel can be seen in Revelation. 22.3. There shall be no more curse manifested in all the earth. God has become all in all Ephesians 1:23b. Therefore it is normal for us to see fruit and healing for all the nations in the end (Revelation 22:2).

God's plan from the beginning, to the middle, to the end was to reverse the curse. Sickness is just part of the poor way the world is today; it is part of the curse. However, it is reversed. Jesus death and resurrection changed everything. If sin is done away with in our life, it is our duty to walk out, to prove, to live out that reality. So in the same way, by God's exact same grace and power we are walk out, prove, live out healing, health, supernatural wholeness.

Some argue that God puts sickness on people for his glory. No, it makes no sense that God gets glory from sickness anymore than God gets glory from sin. God does, however, get glory from healing.

Jews may have thought that people were sick because they were sinful. It is true in the larger sense: sickness came in because of sin. However, we wouldn't want to say, you are sick because you must have sinned. It may be true. It may not be true. Either way, it is does us harm to assume so, and probably a great deal of harm to say so. Sickness is part of the curse, just like sin. So when the Jews asked Jesus who sinned to make the blind man blind, him or his parents, Jesus deflects that way of thinking. He points to thinking, not of the path to find blame, but the path to find God. God healing the man is God's glory. Instead of trying to reason out who is sinful, think of God's goodness, his glory, his grace—and seek that.

Likewise, instead of thinking up reasons why we should resign ourselves to sickness, let us seek God, seek his glory, seek His grace. Likely, in finding our great Father, we will find his great blessings. Nevertheless, let us point our minds to God. This is correct thinking.

Let us not think on the curse, become comfortable with the curse, cuddle up to the curse. No, let us obtain the promise of the blessing. We are blessed with all blessings. Let us lay hold of the promises.

"Swiss Cheese and Look at Him Now!"

I have experienced a real victory in healing with your offspring, particularly with one grandson. My daughter and grandsons were in a terrible accident. I had my hands full. One dead, One on the point of death in a coma and not expected to live, one about to turn 2 with a broken femur and covered in glass, and my daughter in shock, 9 fractures in her face and busted ankle—with no care, because the boys were so bad. What a Christmas present—I had—ice on the highway.

But a good ending. Everybody is great today. A.J.—not expected to live and if he did, to be a vegetable-- will still be the best pitcher of his elementary school team, can read, is doing fine in private school AND ---- made an A in spelling on his report card.—I doubt his mother ever many an A on any spelling test! Yes, my offspring is healed and happy. And grandmother has been changed completely, too.

Let me just tell you about some of the miracles with A.J.

The life-flighted him to the best pediatric ICU in the state. He lay there in the bed, suddenly so very small, shivering, almost dead. His face was smashed into his brain. His face was at first swollen and blue. We prayed at his bed 24 hours.

I did have some help, and I bless and honor those folks who came out, not even knowing us to pray with us—I just called the folks at Kenneth Copeland Ministries—the only people I knew in that town—and some folks gave up their Christmas service to see my daughter and to pray with her. And other ones visited us.

My daughter pinned a handkerchief they gave her to A.J.'s pillow. He laid there, so so small (looking much smaller than 5 years old) , so cold, shivering, and comatose. There was very little consideration for anyone in the family or even AJ from the nursing staff. We had all we could do to keep them from banging heavy equipment against his bed. We had no real info except the monitor. We were careful not to ask for a prognosis. We stayed as deep in prayer, as much as we knew. I shudder to think how little I knew then.

When the staff felt that A.J.s vital signs were stabilized, they called a plastic surgeon in from another hospital to consider how they might put the bones of his face back into position. I saw how deferential the doctors were to this new one. I watched as the surgeons looked at the x-rays on the computer. The surgeon couldn't make sense of what he was seeing. He called for the computer technician. It was no good. Then he called for new x-rays. I was there when the groups was reassembled. The surgeon shook his head. Everyone was silent. Well, you don't need me, he said. His face was back in place and the bones were already farther along in healing than could have been.

One day the nurses put in a Batman movie. With that hand that often flopped A.J. made the Spiderman hand gesture of shooting a web. I started dancing. The nurses ran over to check him, thinking I had gone mad. They soon discovered no radical change and I explained, 'HE Can hear and understand! That is the hand signal he and his brother were doing at my house!" They practically danced with me. That was the first indication I had that they had not expected to see him come out of the coma.

Days later, after he was talking to me (although no one was believing me) I called the trooper who picked up my offspring off the icy road. "Thanks very much" I said. "He is talking? He is talking? He is out of his coma and talking?" I assured him, that yes it was so. "Ma'am, you ought to talk to the medic who worked on your family that day. He said that boy had a zero percent chance of living." "yes, I plan to call him and thank him next. I called the medic next. "just wanted to say thank you and let you know that AJ is out of his coma and talking." The line was completely silent—for a long time. "We believe in miracles, you see." "Yes ma'am." was all he said. I think his voice was breaking. It was the voice of a man who couldn't talk.

Once AJ woke up, there was still a battle of faith. We insisted only positive words be spoken in A.J. hearing We insisted on a positive expectation in a therapy plan—they laughed at us when we said we would take him home walking and talking, and going to the bathroom. They laughed at us when we said weeks. They figured he would leave as a vegetable when benefits ran out in 6 months. He was ready to leave in 2 weeks.

We insisted on no negative words in his room. Fortunately, we prayed for a got a doctor that week who agreed and so it was ordered.

Here I was in the faith battle of my life—no time to doubt, no time to think. The folks from KCM came regularly, and in the process they brought a little book for my daughter. I was waiting in another hospital while she got her ankle pinned back together, so I broke out the book. It was a Sister Copeland's book Blessed Beyond Measure—about how her grandfather just wanted to give stuff to his grandkids. She said God is like that. That wasn't the God I knew about. … I guess I wanted to. I needed to receive. It was a new idea to me. I knew a bunch of Scripture, but the God I thought I knew couldn't be trusted. Here was someone willing to walk through a big trial with me, here was evidence that miracles do happen—of which I had not doubt—so I was willing to give this idea of a good God—a good consideration.

God is good and wants to do us good.

Several weeks later, we drove to a doctor who could take the cast off of the younger boy. We were all cramped in a little exam room: me, my daughter, both grandsons, and my sister, a pediatrician who was introducing us to this new doctor, a friend of hers who would cut off the 3 year old's cast. "Really, I saw the CAT scan. This one had swiss cheese for brains, and look at him now" she said laughing in utter amazement. The other doctor looked skeptical, but happy. That was a reasonable response. My sister wonders if the doctor who said that A.J.'s face was smashed in just made a wrong diagnosis.

My daughter and grandsons were very smashed up; my grandson was pulled back from death into life by the power of faith, and in the process, I was given a book by the folks who were helping us. This young lady who came also gave me this verse of Scripture: Isa 54:13.... All your offspring shall be taught by the LORD and great shall be their shalom.... I had to wrestle a bit -- was this really something I could trust?... Well, yeah, I could accept that it was about more than ancient Israel. I checked the Hebrew—wow! it specifically included grandchildren. I just decided to trust myself to it. I decided to throw myself into it. I decided that this sort of God was worth trusting myself to, once again.

I had to stand in faith through physical therapy. I had to stand in faith through family trials, I had to stand in faith through the homeschooling that brought A.J. up to reading and grade level. Pretty soon, I had to stand in faith for my own finances. Pretty soon I found I was blessed .

It all happened because I had to had to had to have a miracle for my grandson—and I got it.

God is the same God for everyone. God is a good God. God wants to bless, heal, save, and deliver. I want to share my hope with you, so you too have the faith to seeking healing and health, *whether that comes instantaneously or a little more slowly, whether it comes without your intervention or with your witty innovations, or through the help of others*

CHAPTER FIVE

God Wants You Healed.
We Know This From the Nature of God.

God is good. There is no wickedness in God. There is no variation in whether God is good or not. There is no flaw in God's goodness. God is not a "respecter of persons," meaning God does NOT play favorites.

Being well is better, more good, better than being sick.

Therefore God would want you healed, healthy, whole.

This is an important point: that God wants you healed. There have been a lot of lies told about sickness and healing and then ignorantly applied incorrect to the nature of God. So many, even most, of us believe lies about our Father God.

Of course it doesn't help that so very many of us have messed up, irresponsible fathers. Many of us have no idea what a good father would be. God, on the other hand, is a perfect Father.

Good fathers wish the best for their children. And they work to see that it happens. A good father would not hurt his child. He would not put a sickness or an injury on one of his children! Breaking legs doesn't teach. Taking away ability doesn't strengthen. It makes no sense. God des not put sickness on us.

So why do we get sick? Let's see. The world is fallen. *[For those who cannot take this point on faith, let me go the dangerous route of explaining it with reason.] I think everyone would agree that the world is not only good, but mixed with good and evil. Those who see evil as bad and regrettable say the world is broken. I think that is the common experience. So human bodies just have a situation where they can get sick and even die. Then, sometimes, we violate health rules. So when a fifty year old man who is a chain smoker dies of lung cancer, that is not because God struck him down. It is because he lived in a fallen world and didn't take care of his health. So the natural result, however sad to his family and possibly to himself, is that he got sick. Often in today's world it is not so obvious to people how the rules of health were broken because we do of often not know what they are, and our society assumes contrary ideas, but that is a topic for later.

Good fathers wish the best for their children. And they work to see that it happens. They might not be able to keep a child from any and every trouble. But if a child got into trouble, a good and powerful father would have a plan to help the child get out of trouble.

Good fathers wish the best for their children. God is the Perfect Father. Why in the world would there be the idea that God might cause hard things to come upon us? Well, okay, it is possible that God might allow challenges or give us assignments that we find challenging. The Bible indicates we should expect persecutions. I will bet that even Paul might have sometimes chosen to lounge around in his hometown rather than go forth boldly into raucous marketplaces and riled up synagogues. But nowhere does the Bible indicate that God places sickness, disease and such torment upon his children.

Good fathers wish the best for their children. And they work to see that it happens. However, that doesn't mean that the children have to do nothing, for that would not be good fathering, either, now, would it? So let us consider this other argument. A father, under certain circumstances *might* pose a challenge for his son, a task that will strengthen the son and strengthen his muscles, to bring him into responsible manhood. Even allowing for this possibility, I don't see how one could argue that God makes people sick. God might allow a maturing Christian to fall according to his mis-steps: don't sleep, don't eat right, and what do you know, you don't feel good. The challenge then is not the sickness, but the believing for healing. Do you notice that new believers get healed more easily than people who have believed for a long time? Is it God's will? Or is it that after a long time we loose our first love, our first child-like trust and begin to believe a lot of false stories. I don't even know if it is necessary to know the answer to this question in the abstract. The point would be to accept your healing.

Once it was sweetly argued to me that God seems to puts sickness on a believer to strengthen their faith. I might agree that sometimes God permits challenging circumstances so that we develop patience and faith. For instance, we have to be patient with our spouse's spiritual growth, we might have to hold our tongue when someone unjustly criticizes us, or we have to face a scary shortfall in giving in a new ministry we were told to do. Very likely we will experience persecution in some small way because of our dedication to Christ. Those kind of circumstances cause for growth in patience and faith. But sickness? Sickness might call for patience and faith, but would it be GOD that put it on us? First off, while it might seem reasonable to this sister, there simply is no evidence in the Bible that such is the case. Then, following her reasoning, I would suggest that IF God did, then it would be in order for us to believer for our healing. Simply being sick and continuing to be sick does not increase out faith. If what the sister were arguing WERE true, then it would prove my point, because if God wanted to strengthen our faith then He would expect us to believe for healing successfully—to pass the test. Teachers do not give tests that they don't expect their students to pass—if they are trying. Therefore to argue that God places sickness on us makes God a bad father and a poor teacher.

At any rate the Bible teaches contrary. Nowhere does that Bible suggest that God places sickness on believers. There is at least one place it is mentions sickness coming on a person as a judgment. There is lots of evidence, abundant evidence that God wants to heal us, and wants us well, health, and whole. God is good. In him there is no wickedness at all. Therefore God, as the Perfect Father, wishes for and works for all good for His children. The challenges we face are those pulling us from him trying to keep us in the world or those we choose because we are of Him in this world— flesh and persecution— not something he puts on us. Let us see this lie for what it is, confusion and fear. Let us, instead of reasoning with our small minds, run to Our Father, to His Word, to His grace and healing. He wants Great Shalom for His children—beyond what we can imagine.

CHAPTER SIX

God Wants You Well.
We Know This Because God
Does Not Play Favorites

Therefore lay aside lies that come to you either from your own thinking or someone else' and indeed, believe the Word of God. Accept the Good Father's good intention for you; accept the fact that God wants you healed

> Acts 10:34 & 35
> Then Peter opened his mouth, and said, Of a truth I perceive that God is no respecter of persons:
> But in every nation he that feareth him, and worketh righteousness, is accepted with him.

> James 2:1
> My brethren, have not the faith of our Lord Jesus Christ, the Lord of glory, with respect of persons. KJV

> My brothers, as believers in our glorious Lord Jesus Christ, don't show favoritism. NIV

God healed others. God is not "respecter of persons" (James 2:1). This means God does not play favorites. What God will do for one, he will do for another. What God will do for anyone, God will do for you.

Early on, as I was starting out on the path I am walking now, Satan sent a "why didn't my dearest brother get healed' question to me. Of course, I didn't realize at first what was happening. When I eventually answered the question, strongly said that it doesn't work that way, and then stressed God's goodness, suddenly this person who so wanted to keep asking me that question, no longer wanted teaching and it was revealed how wicked a situation it really was. For a while, it looked like I had a couple of guys who wanted to come to my Bible study and who were using my help to reform their lives. But I kept getting contradicted while I taught the Bible. No, this method of evangelism was not okay. No, that Bible was not okay. That teaching was not plain enough. Then somehow the Bible Study was not convenient enough. Was I doing it badly? How could I accommodate these guys more? Surely this fellow had experience; maybe I should see things his way. What really got me the most was this insistent question about why God heals some and not others. There was a heart wrenching story, so I really cared. In the meantime, someone else let me in on the fact that this supposedly holy person who felt he could tell me how to and how not to teach was living a lifestyle that was frightening in the extreme. I had not and wouldn't go along with "God just won't heal some people," "Why isn't God fair?" and this insinuation, like a Nazgul knife, that God plays favorites. When I finally drew a line in the sand over that, proposed to teach directly on this, that had been asked so many times, these fellows were not interested in meeting with me any more. "No, we just want to spend time with you (and keep asking you this why God doesn't heal the best people, even though our original agreement was to come to your Bible Study.) I am always ready to help someone with the Word of God who is trying to pull themselves out of the mire by it. I think, however, this couple, these two fellows, might have been on assignment to take me out, take my faith out, by pulling on my heartstrings this story.

Guess what, even if the story were true, that some guy who was a good Christian and lived perfectly ended up dying, guess what, he went to heaven and feels pretty well healed now. It just is not my business to know everyone else's life. I am just not interested in "but what if." I am interested, however, in agreements being kept. So if you want to come to my Bible Study, come and let's study the Bible.

Eventually, in retrospect, I realized that every time I had accommodated these guys in backing up from what I had been felt God wanted me to teach, muting what I was supposed to teach, I was accommodating the Devil!

This is how lies work. They sneak up on you. They suggest that you should be more reasonable. They suggest you should have more pity. They distract you from the Word of God. They do not, however, bear scrutiny. Write out the challenge. Find out the assumptions and presumptions. Then write out the Word of God that relates. You will find that other scriptures will knock down the presuppositions and axioms on which the propositions are based. You will find, also, that empirical evidence is at least as much on the side of the Word of God.

It appears that all of reality is on the natural side and on the other, the Word of God is asking you to believe something fantastical, unbelievable, and unreasonable. But if you check things out, you will find this is an illusion. Experience of reliable witnesses and often even the best of science often lines up with the Word. Even if it didn't, I'd rather be on the side of the One who created the world, built the ethic system, and will judge the whole shebang at the end—especially if this One presents his intentions as miraculously good. What is to doubt?

God healed people in the Old Testament. God healed people in the New Testament. God healed various people of various ailments in various ways. God is still healing today. This same God who heals speaks to us and spoke to many who recorded it in the Bible. God does not play favorites. God is everlasting the same. God does have principles. They are principles rooted in God's divine nature. God is love.

Thus, once again I say, God wants you healed.

Healed of Internal Torment

They said it was a result of the accident. They called it trauma. I was over the initial healing period. I was back to work. I still had a little getting stronger to do. I had moved away to another town. I was without income. I was filling myself with Word. Still, I had a nagging fear. I did consult my doctor and did everything he said. Still I fought it. It was a great tutor—I studied faith diligently.

Years before I had fought depression. Never would I have given in. Never would I have stayed in bed. Never would I have missed work. Never would I have slackened my goals. Never would I have taken psychotropic drugs. But I had perused the shelves of the health food store. I had to drag myself along. I was heroically facing a life that was needlessly and annoyingly difficult, it seemed to me.

I remember wondering, just once, whether I were cursed. So many years of poverty. So few relationship that worked out. So much character, so much intelligence, so much application—and an unimaginably little to show for it. I only had to wonder once, then I ran to the arms of God.

Even in the arms of God, I had to diligently look to God, not at myself. I went forward. I filled myself with God's promises. And increasingly with God's assignments. And you know, one day I turned around and discovered that far from being fearful, I was fearless. I discovered far from being depressed, I was buoyant even in very trying situations.

My struggles with emotion are perhaps not much compared to others. Or perhaps they are just as much as others, but my thinking doesn't allow me to wallow in nonsense like "you can't change how you feel" because of course you can. Nor would I resign myself to having an illness. I have no way of knowing how my experience compares to others'. I cannot compare. All I know is this: God is SO good. God makes me happy. God set me free from what could have been torment.

I see friends tormented. I know one who has talked to me more than once about the possibility of being cursed. I know others who have succumbed to taking psychotropic drugs. Still others have been hospitalized. None of these friends have been willing to talk with me about surrender to Jesus; none of them has been willing to feed themselves a diet of faith, none ran to God. I suspect that God can heal internal ailments just as well as external.

CHAPTER SEVEN

God Wants You Healed.
We Know This from the Experience
of the Early Church

Mark 6:56
And whithersoever he entered, into villages, or cities, or country, they laid the sick in the streets, and besought him that they might touch if it were but the border of his garment: and as many as touched him were made whole.

Acts 5: 12-20

12 And by the hands of the apostles were many signs and wonders wrought among the people; (and they were all with one accord in Solomon's porch.

13 And of the rest durst no man join himself to them: but the people magnified them.

14 And believers were the more added to the Lord, multitudes both of men and women.)

15 Insomuch that they brought forth the sick into the streets, and laid them on beds and couches, that at the least the shadow of Peter passing by might overshadow some of them.

16 There came also a multitude out of the cities round about unto Jerusalem, bringing sick folks, and them which were vexed with unclean spirits: and they were healed every one.

17 Then the high priest rose up, and all they that were with him, (which is the sect of the Sadducees,) and were filled with indignation,

18 And laid their hands on the apostles, and put them in the common prison.

19 But the angel of the Lord by night opened the prison doors, and brought them forth, and said,

20 Go, stand and speak in the temple to the people all the words of this life.

In Acts 5:15 we see that healing was a regular experience. People not in the close fellowship, not coming to preaching meetings were aware of the healing power of Christ through the Holy Spirit that rest on the Peter—and the other apostles, seeing that the authorities wanted more than Peter arrested (v18.). They brought their sick into the streets where the apostles walked. Think about what that means. People not in the church, learned enough about what was going on that they would go out of their way to get some of the healing given out by God through the disciples. They even came from other cities. They would take their sick loved ones into street—at that time filled with excrement of transport animals and often humans— in order to find wholeness. If healing power in the church was this well known in the city, what must have been happening in the church?

"Is any among you afflicted? Let him pray. Is any merry? Let him sing psalms," (James 5:13). That was the normal instruction. But there is more:

James 5

14 Is any sick among you? Let him call for the elders of the church; and let them pray over him, anointing him with oil in the name of the Lord:

15 And the prayer of faith shall save the sick, and the Lord shall raise him up; and if he have committed sins, they shall be forgiven him.

16 Confess your faults one to another, and pray one for another, that ye may be healed. The effectual fervent prayer of a righteous man availeth much.

In James 5:14 The apostle James, considered, the head minister for a time in Jerusalem, writes that "IF anyone is sick… " I note the IF.

Today, a bishop would write 'when…" or "if you feel the power, then…" because any congregation of any size today will have someone sick or someone with a loved one very sick. James writes, "IF any is sick..." then here is what to do... The elders should pray and anoint with oil. Then the sick believer will recover.

The discussion of liberal scholars about whether this anointing with oil meant administration of medicine is not helpful. It may be that oil was used within medicine at that time. It may be that today God will bless the practice of medicine, alternative or allopathic. I do not see command the believer to abstain from medical treatment as a blanket rule. However, anointing was a spiritual expression from the time of the anointing of Aaron and his sons, the anointing of David as King, to the very name of the word Messiah. It indicates the power of the Holy Spirit. I am suggesting it is simply unbelieving to read this as command people to use medicine rather than prayer in this verse, when clearly the Holy Spirit's power is what is meant. This is exactly the kind of contribution from theologians that gets them preached against.

Oil is placed on the believer as a visible, tangible sign, a point of contact, of the Holy Spirit's power being on the believer for healing. I wonder if it is not is one of God's methods for crossing from the absolute to the contingent, from the spiritual to the natural, from eternity to time.

Then James says, he, the believer SHALL be raised up. Never in medicine do we so positively affirm the result. Therefore this verse is NOT about medicine; it is about the power of the Holy Spirit. The believer shall be raised up. Using *shall* with the 3rd person in English means a very definite affirmation: *most certainly* will be raised up. In other words, those going down to death will definitely be raised up in life. Sound familiar? If we believe in the resurrection, how could we not believe in healing?

Healing was the expectation of the early church. Their experience, their expectation is clearly recorded in black and white.

Paul, similarly, shows his expectations. He also expects a healed, healthy church. However, in the first letter to the church at Corinth, he had to explain the opposite: sickness and death. The very fact he has to explain shows that the opposite, healing and health, was expected.

Corinthians 11:29-31

29 For he that eateth and drinketh unworthily, eateth and drinketh damnation to himself, not discerning the Lord's body.

30 For this cause many are weak and sickly among you, and many sleep.

31 For if we would judge ourselves, we should not be judged.

His words, however, were a warning in a letter where he correct several other disorders in a congregation. The Corinthians were riddled with division and strife, someone was involved in serious sexual disorder, and there was even some confusion about how to run services. In this congregation they experienced sickness and death. Even in this situation of a messed up congregation, the situation of sickness was puzzling enough that an apostle would take the time to explain why it existed.

It was the experience and expectation of the early church to have believer healed, rescued, made whole, by the power of the Holy Spirit.

Therefore don't be unbelieving, accepting stories about the anointing as it if were ignorant people talking ineptly about medicine. Do not accept stories that God might not want your healed. Paul says you most certainly shall be raised up. Do not accept a story about spirituality as if sickness and death were a sentence upon everyone and resurrection were a fairy story. Do not accept reasonable stories that are contrary to clear words in Scriptures such as I Peter 2:24 "by whose stripes ye were healed."

Healing was the expectation and experience of the early church. You are not a bit different than those believers. The world and the church has changed, admittedly. God certainly hasn't changed. The Word hasn't changed— except that we have the New Testament written down for us. Therefore accept, take hold of, and believe that God wants you healed.

I Stood for a Long Time,
I Prayed More than Once,
Then I Rejoiced

Last week, I left the driveway, whooping down the driveway, because I received a healing I had been waiting on for some months. I had a sore spot on my gum. I had carried out the health measures I knew. I went to the altar of the church where I was visiting, both believing in healing and knowing they were having some succeed in that area. That was Spring 07. In Fall 07, in the church where I now go, the pastor had us get in small groups and pray for each other during the praise service. (We have not done that before or since and indeed, I think he got the idea from the pastor at the church where I was visiting.) I felt I had faith, knew I believed in healing, and didn't know much about the women with me. A sister, a pillar of the church, prayed for me. I felt heat on me. I know it was the power of God. However, my gum remained the same. I thanked God and stood in healing whenever I thought about it.

I applied more health food type measures, diligently.

By spring 2008, I was concerned and even mentioned it to my doctor. He was more concerned, ordered me to the dentist, and gave me words of warning. A few weeks after that, I was feeling that the business and cares of this life had put a dull edge on my ardor and prayer life. I went to church early, indeed, had to wait for the doors to be opened, so I could have my full prayer time before service. I had a good time with God. I transacted a lot of business with the Lord. Among other things, I reminded God about my gum. Monday, I noticed that my gum sore was half gone. Friday, I looked, with the feeling like I have about memories long ago. I saw that my gum sore what completely gone. It was a week of miracles, and I whooped going out of the driveway to work. Bring on the blessings! Bring on the advancement!

CHAPTER EIGHT

God Wants You Healed.
We Know this Because God Said So.
God is the creator

Isaiah 40:28
Hast thou not known? hast thou not heard, that the everlasting God, the LORD, the Creator of the ends of the earth, fainteth not, neither is weary? there is no searching of his understanding.

Isaiah 44:24
Thus saith the LORD, thy redeemer, and he that formed thee from the womb, I am the LORD that maketh all things; that stretcheth forth the heavens alone; that spreadeth abroad the earth by myself;

1 Peter 4:19
Wherefore let them that suffer according to the will of God commit the keeping of their souls to him in well doing, as unto a faithful Creator.

God is good

Psalm 73:1
Truly God is good to Israel, even to such as are of a clean heart

Psalm 109:21
But do thou for me, O GOD the Lord, for thy name's sake: because thy mercy is good, deliver thou me.

Psalm 25:8
Good and upright is the LORD: therefore will he teach sinners in the way.

Psalm 5:4
For thou art not a God that hath pleasure in wickedness: neither shall evil dwell with thee.

God has good intentions toward us

Jeremiah 29:11
11 'For I know the plans that I have for you,' declares the LORD, 'plans for welfare and not for calamity to give you a future and a hope. NASB

Psalm 84:11
For the LORD God is a sun and shield: the LORD will give grace and glory: no good thing will he withhold from them that walk uprightly

Isaiah 61:1
The Spirit of the Lord GOD is upon me; because the LORD hath anointed me to preach good tidings unto the meek; he hath sent me to bind up the brokenhearted, to proclaim liberty to the captives, and the opening of the prison to them that are bound;

God claims to be our healer

Exodus 15:26
And said, If thou wilt diligently hearken to the voice of the LORD thy God, and wilt do that which is right in his sight, and wilt give ear to his commandments, and keep all his statutes, I will put none of these diseases upon thee, which I have brought upon the Egyptians: for I am the LORD that healeth thee.

Psalm 41: 3
3 The LORD will sustain him on his sickbed
and restore him from his bed of illness. NIV

God is the redeemer, deliverer

2 Samuel 22:2
And he said, The LORD is my rock, and my fortress, and my deliverer

Psalm 18:2
The LORD is my rock, and my fortress, and my deliverer; my God, my strength, in whom I will trust; my buckler, and the horn of my salvation, and my high tower.

Psalm 34:6
This poor man cried, and the LORD heard him, and saved him out of all his troubles.

Psalm 40:17
But I am poor and needy; yet the Lord thinketh upon me: thou art my help and my deliverer; make no tarrying, O my God.

Isaiah 41:14
Fear not, thou worm Jacob, and ye men of Israel; I will help thee, saith the LORD, and thy redeemer, the Holy One of Israel.

Isaiah 54:5 & 8
For thy Maker is thine husband; the LORD of hosts is his name; and thy Redeemer the Holy One of Israel; The God of the whole earth shall he be called.God promises and does not lie ….
In a little wrath I hid my face from thee for a moment; but with everlasting kindness will I have mercy on thee, saith the LORD thy Redeemer.

God's Promises are Sure

Deuteronomy 31:6
Be strong and of a good courage, fear not, nor be afraid of them: for the LORD thy God, he it is that doth go with thee; he will not fail thee, nor forsake thee.

Numbers 23:19
God is not a man, that he should lie; neither the son of man, that he should repent: hath he said, and shall he not do it? or hath he spoken, and shall he not make it good?

Isaiah 55:11
11 So shall my word be that goeth forth out of my mouth: it shall not return unto me void, but it shall accomplish that which I please, and it shall prosper in the thing whereto I sent it.

Jeremiah 1:12
Then said the LORD unto me, Thou hast well seen: for I will hasten my word to perform it.

Certainly will God Give You Good Things

Luke 11:11
If a son shall ask bread of any of you that is a father, will he give him a stone? or if he ask a fish, will he for a fish give him a serpent?
Have tasted that god is gracious. I Pe 2:3

Romans 8:32
He that spared not his own Son, but delivered him up for us all, how shall he not with him also freely give us all things?
How will he not give us freely of all things?

God would like to keep you well

Exodus 15:26
And said, If thou wilt diligently hearken to the voice of the LORD thy God, and wilt do that which is right in his sight, and wilt give ear to his commandments, and keep all his statutes, I will put none of these diseases upon thee, which I have brought upon the Egyptians: for I am the LORD that healeth thee.

Psalm 67:2
That thy way may be known upon earth, thy saving health among all nations.

Proverbs 3:8
It shall be health to thy navel, and marrow to thy bones.

Proverbs 4:22
For they are life unto those that find them, and health to all their flesh.

Proverbs 12:18
There is that speaketh like the piercings of a sword: but the tongue of the wise is health.

3 John 1:2
Beloved, I wish above all things that thou mayest prosper and be in health, even as thy soul prospereth.

God has promised health

Isaiah 58:8
Then shall thy light break forth as the morning, and thine health shall spring forth speedily: and thy righteousness shall go before thee; the glory of the LORD shall be thy reward.

Jeremiah 33:6

Behold, I will bring it health and cure, and I will cure them, and will reveal unto them the abundance of peace and truth.

God said he has healed you

Isaiah 53:5

But he was wounded for our transgressions, he was bruised for our iniquities: the chastisement of our peace was upon him; and with his stripes we are healed.

James 5:16

Confess your faults one to another, and pray one for another, that ye may be healed. The effectual fervent prayer of a righteous man availeth much.

1 Peter 2:24

Who his own self bare our sins in his own body on the tree, that we, being dead to sins, should live unto righteousness: by whose stripes ye were healed.

We receive it

Jeremiah 17:14

Heal me, O LORD, and I shall be healed; save me, and I shall be saved: for thou art my praise.

Hebrews 4:1, 15 & 16

1 Let us therefore fear, lest, a promise being left us of entering into his rest, any of you should seem to come short of it…Seeing then that we have a great high priest, that is passed into the heavens, Jesus the Son of God, let us hold fast our profession…

15. For we have not an high priest which cannot be touched with the feeling of our infirmities; but was in all points tempted like as we are, yet without sin.

16 Let us therefore come boldly unto the throne of grace, that we may obtain mercy, and find grace to help in time of need.

Revelation 22:20
He which testifieth these things saith, Surely I come quickly. Amen. *Even so, come, Lord Jesus.*

A Healing Legacy?

Last Thursday, I had to call my daughter for a piece of business information. Immediately, I heard a unusual sounds.

"Where are you?"

"The emergency room."

"Who is hurt?"

"A.J. He hurt his thumb playing ball."

"May I speak with him please?"

"Hi Grandmother; my thumb is broke."

"Are you sure, A.J.?"

"Oh, it's broke."

"Well, you remember that God healed you, don't you? God fixed your bones then. You know God loves you, right? You know God can heal you right? Can we pray for your healing now? Okay, Dear Lord, thank you that you love A.J. Thank you that you have healed him before. Thank you that Jesus paid the full price for everything, for our salvation, for taking care of us, and for healing. We claim this thumb fixed, in Jesus name."

"Okay, now I have to talk to the doctor, Grandmother."

"Say AMEN!"

"Amen! Bye."

I think that is about what I prayed.

My daughter says that the x-rays showed that the thumb was not broken. She said that since the thumb was clearly bent in a way that thumbs don't go, then it must have been dislocated. But why, I ask, would a dislocated thumb not hurt? My elementary school aged grandson was completely sure that his thumb was in fact broken. That was Thursday night. Saturday, the thumb is fine, completely fine. Even a dislocated thumb wouldn't be completely fine on Saturday, I don't think. This is miracle enough for this Grandmother.

Incidentally, the next piece of business for me that night was to call friends in that same town. I wanted to offer them the new CD set on Healing from Bill Johnson. Did they want it? OH YES! And sorry, Sharon, we cannot talk a long time, we are running off to the hospital. Oh, how are your family? Okay, we will visit them.

That is too much of a coincidence in a week of miracles to be a coincidence in my mind!.

Certainly R. W. Schambach can tell you greater stories. He had a man come back to life in a revival. He saw a little baby that was blind, deaf, twisted, with no feet, in one of his meeting, before their yes, gain sight, untwist, grow feet, and walk away. Bill Johnson and his students have found victory over cancer, multiple sclerosis and many other diseases Todd Bentley sees healing signs and wonders that convent whole villages in Africa. Pastor Benny Hinn has hundreds, perhaps thousands, healed in miracle crusades every month. I am ready to learn from these guys. But maybe you, like my friends, would be instructed by a normal mother and grandmother. My friends know about these guys. They know of the teaching of Kenneth Hagin and Kenneth and Gloria Copeland and their friends. Nevertheless, one day I found myself strongly discussing with them that God always wants to heal. So I wrote this book for them, and friends I don't know, just like them, just like you. God wants you healed! Please let your faith be stirred and strengthened. God wants your and your children healed, whole, healthy, and in great shalom.

CHAPTER NINE

God Wants Your Children Healed, Whole And Healthy, Too.

God wants to heal always, just as God want everyone to be saved. God wants you healed. He wants your children healed too. Never forget it.

If I have burst any arguments, this is the argument that I most wish to burst: this idea that because something is "genetic" that we must resign ourselves to it. First, the whole idea of "genetic" being the reason is often not reasonable. Children have all kinds of problems today that are labeled "genetic" that in fact are not. Even if a problem indeed is "genetic" that is, runs in the family, why should that condition suddenly be exempt? Is "genetic" a higher name than God's? No, in fact generational curses are overtaken and reversed by generational Blessings from Our Father and our Big Brother. Our bloodline is the blood of Christ Jesus. Our inheritance is far higher than we imagine. The Holy Spirit is the down payment!

I have had it with this resignation. It is merely accepting a lie. It is lying down for a lie to walk on you. People talk to me like I don't know what these ailments are. I am not immune to ailments. I know healing. And I know health. So why does that make me somehow too stupid to have understood what ailment you are talking about? Would it help you if you know how far I had gone down that road? Very unlikely will I tell you if I had. Why should I exalt that?

It is like, I know how not to drink. That in itself might make me a good resource for someone who doesn't know now not to drink. If I knew how to drink and stopped, then that also makes me a good resource. Your knowing how badly I drank in times past might not. But people who drink might like to discount my experience because I am not so bad off as them. Hmm. Hmpf.

Well I never had a problem with alcohol, but I have been sick. Fortunately, however, I learned about healing when I was young. So, no, I don't have stories of large sicknesses. But that doesn't make me a write off!

I do have stories about my family having large injuries. I do have large healing stories. I will share those safely away from those little ears. For now and the future, however, I would prefer to claim security and safety for those loved ones, and not more healing stories.

I should be used to being written off. I will however, argue against this: this resignation that writes off God's desire to heal you and your children. Most people believe that God COULD heal if he wanted to. I hope I have established in your mind that indeed, GOD DOES WANT TO—in fact God already did something—because God wants you healed.

I want to go further. God wants to heal your child. More children today than every before have some sort of problem. The rapid and dramatic rise of incidence and prevalence of most of these problems suggest that there are things we can do to prevent them and possibly reverse them. Others are researching and promulgating these initiatives. If we are overloading the human system with toxins, poor nutrition, polluted EM environment, and polluted social environment then it is good that we know it, so we can reverse our behavior. Let's talk about that another time.

The root, the ultimate cause, and the ultimate cure is what I am talking about. God is present to rescue, to save, and to heal. That is what deliverance means. That is what salvation means—full *shalom*.

For the present, if you have a child who has problem, please reach out to the same God, the same Creator, the same Perfect parent, the same healer, the same Jesus, Holy Spirit, present in power to heal. (Lu 9:2 & 11) The promises are to you and to your children (Acts 2:39).

Salvation comes to your whole household.

Acts 16:15
And when she was baptized, and her household, she besought us,

saying, If ye have judged me to be faithful to the Lord, come into my house, and abide there. And she constrained us.

Acts 16:31
And they said, Believe on the Lord Jesus Christ, and thou shalt be saved, and thy house.

Psalm 103:17
 17 But the mercy of the LORD is from everlasting to everlasting upon them that fear him, and his righteousness unto children's children;

Israel, into whom we are grafted, as we are in Christ by faith, is specifically promised:

Isaiah 54:13
 13 And all thy children shall be taught of the LORD; and great shall be the peace of thy children. KJV

And all your offspring(children and grandchildren shall be taught of the LORD, and great shall be the shalom of your offspring. (my own translation)

Salvation is shalom, not just rescue, but perfect well-being, nothing missing nothing broken.

Psalm 115:14
The LORD shall increase you more and more, you and your children.

Teach this to your children. Bless your children. Claim healing for your children. Teach them to stay in contact with God, claim healing, and walk always in health. Please notice Deuteronomy in the sixth chapter, the passage most dear to our Jewish brothers. Here the Lord tells us to teach our children. Notice the context of blessings promised.

Deuteronomy

4 Hear, O Israel: The LORD our God is one LORD:

5 And thou shalt love the LORD thy God with all thine heart, and with all thy soul, and with all thy might.

6 And these words, which I command thee this day, shall be in thine heart:

7 And thou shalt teach them diligently unto thy children, and shalt talk of them when thou sittest in thine house, and when thou walkest by the way, and when thou liest down, and when thou risest up.

8 And thou shalt bind them for a sign upon thine hand, and they shall be as frontlets between thine eyes.

9 And thou shalt write them upon the posts of thy house, and on thy gates.

10 And it shall be, when the LORD thy God shall have brought thee into the land which he sware unto thy fathers, to Abraham, to Isaac, and to Jacob, to give thee great and goodly cities, which thou buildedst not,

11 And houses full of all good things, which thou filledst not, and wells digged, which thou diggedst not, vineyards and olive trees, which thou plantedst not; when thou shalt have eaten and be full;

Our house is to be one marked by the Word of God. Our rearing of our children is filled with daily teaching of God's ways. Thus our house will be blessed, our children greatly blessed.

Sanctify them by the truth; your word is truth.- John 17:17

This suggests to me that if I surround my children with the Word in the right spirit, they can be sanctified. As they are under my care, it is my privilege and right, as well as duty to provide for them as enriched and secure environment as possible. Let them have the birthright of the family: Blessings beyond anything we can imagine, Shalom in connection with The Father.

Matthew 19:14
But Jesus said, Suffer little children, and forbid them not, to come unto me: for of such is the kingdom of heaven.

Mark 10:14
But when Jesus saw it, he was much displeased, and said unto them, Suffer the little children to come unto me, and forbid them not: for of such is the kingdom of God.

Luke 18:16
But Jesus called them unto him, and said, Suffer little children to come unto me, and forbid them not: for of such is the kingdom of God.

Still today, Jesus says, "let the little children come to me." All of these promises, these truths, these realities apply to children and especially your children. Read these passages for yourself. Read them over again, meditating them and claiming them for your children. Teach them to your children. Then the little children will lead us, with childlike faith, receiving from the hand of the Perfect Father, His great good will for us.

Conclusion

Once again, I say, there is no reason to doubt that God wants us healed, both us and our children—and even those outside—for healing is a sign and a wonder. Jesus never turned anyone away. Let's explode the stories that look like they are soothing disappointment but are really lies about God's intentions. God has extended this gift to us. Let us be diligent to receive that gift. Let us take hold. Let's unwrap it. Let's thank our perfect Father for his great gift, thank our older brother for transferring so great a blessing to us, and invite the Holy Spirit in to help us understand, know, and receive.

Great Shalom Broadcast
ORDER FORM

Free ebooks
How to Have a Smarter Baby . . . . .email info@greatshalom.org
Claiming Great Shalom: A Parent's Month of Prayers . .email info@greatshalom.org
Twenty Blessings for Teachers . . . . .email info@greatshalom.org

Booklets and Reports
Seven Keys to Loving Discipline $10.00
Report on Reading: With Special Attention to English
    Spelling and Pronunciation Patterns $10.00

Books
How to Win the Game of School
    (for junior/community college students) $20.00
    on CD or diskette $10.00
Learn at Home for Great Shalom (forthcoming)

Early Childhood Development —4 self- study courses,
Recognized by the Texas Department of Family and Protective Services for continuing education clock hours.
    Introduction to the Montessori Method . . . . .10.00 _____
    Self Esteem for Preschoolers. . . . . .10.00 _____
    Games that Teach for Preschoolers. . . . . .10.00 _____
    Handling Diversity in the Preschool Classroom . . . . 10.00 _____

Postage and handling for first item . . . . $2.00 _____
For each additional item . . . .$1.00 _____
Texas residents add applicable sales tax . . . . .8.25% _____

                                           TOTAL $_____

Make check payable to
Organizational Strategies
P.O. Box 971 • Austin, TX 78630

Ship to:

Name: _____

Address: _____

City: _____

State: _____

Zip: _____

 email: _____

# of items _____ $ _____ enclosed

www.ingramcontent.com/pod-product-compliance
Lightning Source LLC
Chambersburg PA
CBHW031332040426

42443CB00005B/311